# A Book of Poetry

Barry Williams

First published in 2019 by Paragon Publishing, Rothersthorpe
© Barry Williams 2019

ISBN 978-1-78222-678-9

Book design, layout and production management by Into Print
www.intoprint.net
+44 (0)1604 832149

For Dad who continues to inspire me.

# Introduction

I have been writing poetry for the last six years, I mostly put my work up on Social Media, but now I have decided to publish a book.

I get inspiration for my Poetry for world events, News and my own experiences, I first got the idea for writing when I was at work one day and been in a job that never really challenging, my mind wandering back to my School days and apart from thinking where it all went wrong, a particular memory stood out in my mind,

In most English classes the Teacher we had at the time was a big fan of poetry, at the time I found it boring, but, also something sank in and in the days since I have put a verse or two together, Poetry for me gets it said like no other way to write and get what you are trying to get across to the reader.

I have also went back to school and got on an Adult Back to Education course, the course was very helpful in the writing of my book and the it opened up several options available on Micro Soft Word, which I didn't know about and gave me a whole new insight into writing, filing and storing my work on software than actually hand writing everything and having to physically file each and every page, this I found to be invaluable.

So, since the first time I penned my first poetry, it got great reaction on Social Media, so, I thought why not get the message across to those who do not frequent the Information Super Highway, Everyone who is anyone loves to read Poetry and it speaks volumes and sinks in to both mind body and soul and I do hope on occasion it touches your heart as the reader.

To conclude I am Dedicating this Book to My Dear old Dad who passed away in November 2018, he will always be on my mind and in my heart.

# Dad. 1936-2018

You helped us into this world,
Faced all challenges that unfurled,
Always a kind word to ease the pain,
No matter what our story, you listened and never in vain,
You were there through all our first steps,
And reassured when doubt was in reps,
A voice that would shake the ground when we got out of line,
And to hear you sing was just sublime,
You coached us through all our fields of play,
Even had time for a kind word at the end of a busy day,
Off in the car and in to town,
You wouldn't see any sad face frown,
Brought us up right to just be nice,
For the night out you always made up the price,
In the farming years we all helped out,
The machinery got swore at and even the odd clout,
Taught to stand on our own two feet,
Told us doesn't make you any less of a man when you can
admit defeat,
Gave us the choice to choose our own profession,
Now our hearts are in recession,
We pay tribute to only man that we as men admire the most,
May the almighty keep you his heavenly host,
For we are heartbroken and it's plain to see,
Also proud we are our Dads lasting legacy.

# A Different Kind of Christmas

In this year that may not have being kind,
Some Yule tide spirit you may struggle to find,
As most of you who rush around to prepare the food,
For some it's difficult to get in the mood,
For all the years come flooding back,
This one falls short, something does lack,
Put on a brave face and muster a smile,
Keep your chin up that's the style,
For the want to join in and feel the festive zest,
We think of those who have gone to their rest,
Not to be the one who dampens the spirit,
Just to be mindful of those we respect with such merit,
If we could change our life for just one day,
What would be the one thing we would say,
Look to the heavens with a hopeful stare,
It would be nice not to have that empty chair.

# Gone On

So begins the winter of our discontent,
Emotions wrenched of days that were spent,
We gaze upon uncertain days ahead,
Hearts now weep for the one who has fled,
He who now soars oft in the stilly night,
Soul that lingers in hoovering flight,
To watch over the living and those to pass,
On the shore of grief we now mass,
The one who set the pace and laid down the rules,
His legacy now that eternity fuels,
You may be out of sight but, never out of mind,
Memories roar from the depths that grind,
The laughs and tears and the odd row,
Will never fade in silent reflection we will always bow,
It past by so fast in the blink of an eye,
You now reside on most high,
You have travelled beyond the physical being,
Everywhere we turned we think we are seeing,
The man who gave us life and we shared this time and space,
The Father is the one who sets the standard and we inherit the
absent face.

# Father

The day we lifted you shoulder high,
A pride we can't deny,
On that solemn day,
We thought grief would never give way,

We may not be able to see you,
You'll always have the view,
Of the man that we take after,
Through tears and joys of laughter,

You peacefully slipped away,
With no more to say,
The lessons in life are fully taught,
The goal you always sought,

Scrolling through our memory bank,
The day all our hearts sank,
Now you are free to roam,
Ever since that day, the day the Almighty called you home.

# CONTENTS

# The Social Media Years

# Programmed

We do things without conscious thought,
The daily goal is constantly sought,
Are we on auto pilot to get it done,
Want a result second to none,

Can we hit reset when it all goes wrong?
Or sing it off with a mournful song,
Do we live in an age swearing by what it says on a screen?
Blinded by what is unseen,

Better off not knowing what lies beyond,
Of been in charge we have grown quite fond,
Do we go into meltdown when the computer says no?
Enjoy what is in the programmed show,

The tech has now been inserted in our daily routine,
To get in front of it we have gotten quite keen,
Lift our heads to glance the world going by,
But, it's for the good of mankind, so why should we deny.

Didn't read the instructions thought I'd give them a miss,
Carry on in the unrelenting bliss,
Did I do my part in easing mankind along,
Never judge and first do no wrong,

Go through the days like revolving doors,
How many footprints cover these floors,
For I am not alone in this timeless quest,
Asking immortality to be my guest,

So shuffling by on this busy road,
To the endless routine I commend this ode,
What is our greatest fear,
That time would erase what I have done here.

# Reflection

When you think about the time that's being,
Are you caught up in what is done and seen,
Did I do it right and finish the task,
Done my best what more could one ask,

Was there enough time allotted to get it done,
From early morning to the setting of the sun,
Thinking of others along my path,
Slammed the door or set out the welcome mat,

Is the result all that counted,
On the back of this noble steed that I mounted,
Was the payoff good or non-existent,
Wanted to walk away or saw it through by being persistent,

If this was another time and place,
A canter or gallop in this daily race,
Carrying on what has being done through the ages,
Written in stone or faded pages,

I'm not referring to the ceasing of that all-important wage,
That's competitive and often cause for rage,
Looking deeper and beyond that daily quest,
I simply left my abode and became the days honoured guest.

# Pay It Forward

In this circle we call life,
Full of ups and downs, trouble and strife,
Head focused get in the game,
If it all goes wrong where to point the finger of blame,

We strive to keep up appearances,
That well earned money with easy clearances,
Do we have to keep up with Mr. and Mrs Jones,
Graft our bodies to the bones,

Looking towards the end of the week,
Survival of the fittest and not for the meek,
Are we programmed to be this way,
Keep our failures quashed and at bay,

We are all humans and it's not a race,
Saying that it's about credibility and saving face,
Conversation is killed by media overdose,
Get those pictures up, smile don't be morose,

In the heel of the hunt we all finish,
If we're not winning our dreams diminish,
It's borrowed time so live with compassion,
Just do your best with your daily ration,

We all owe to someone and have to pay it on,
Then pass it on to the next generation when we're all dead and
gone,
It's not so morbid if you stop and think,
Consider the passed by because one day it's all gone in a blink.

# Pausing For Thought
*Remembering an old friend*

It's been five years since you were taken away,
As the news filtered through on that ill-fated day,
That feeling that can be felt even now,
Death is as greedy as a crow behind a plough,

In our little community another neighbour laid to rest,
All full of life, vigour and zest,
Personalities that shone through into immortality,
It's always a bitter dose of harsh reality,

To mark the day of your anniversary,
Seems almost like a battle of adversary,
It's said god only takes the chosen few,
Leaves us with only memories in our minds to review,

When we once thought you would out live us all,
It came sudden and brutal, that cruel call,
Why these events ever take place,
Just sit and ponder into the past we must trace,

Then there are friends who enrich our lives,
Then those who define in memorandum we strive,
Alas to have you back to say how much you meant,
A day in a life that was heaven sent,

In hearts and minds and the odd prayer,
Remembering the good times with that unique personalised
flare,
Although it's sad to lose a good friend,
The universe sends the best on loan or just to lend,

In time you will be part of people's stories,
Trails and tribulations and the odd few glories,

Now the future is never really set,
The times we spent we'll never forget,
There are three little girls about their dad they will be told,
Told it all from the brave to the bold!

# Ode To The Seafarer

I went to see the man on the boat,
Asked him how he stayed afloat,
He said with a discerning grin,
I'm the best sea fairer there's ever been,

In high winds   and in frightening gales,
It's good to know when to leave them down or put up your
sails,
Weather the storm and put your faith in God,
To return to the shore and put your feet on the sod.

To have the freedom at your fingertips,
Mistakes are made when the concentration slips,
To be on the ocean wave not a care in the world,
Can't beat the feeling when the sea unfurls,

To be on land I just can't wait,
Get back on the wave without debate,
The scent of the ocean fills the senses,
Give me the sea where there are no picket fences.

# Observations

To ponder into the great beyond,
Does your vision ripple like a disturbed pond?
Following through the passage of time,
Separating the ridiculous from the sublime,

To go forward in the direction you are blown,
Are you armed with what you have carefully sown?
Take that step and go to the breach,
It's about the journey not the destination to reach,

You don't see the danger ahead,
If it all goes wrong were you mislead,
It's all knowledge and what you have learned,
That road got rocky seeking what you have always yearned.

# Not Very Different

From time to time we all think we are unique,
For approval we constantly aim to seek,
Thrown together on this rock,
In not meeting our standards we tend to knock,
When we have a loss we rally around,
A hand of support is out reached with no sound,
Comforting words are said in sincerity,
For grief often comes in all forms of dexterity,
Defiance is in abundance wrong we will refuse,
A brief nod of the head when our team lose,
When life spins out of control,
Sends a shiver to our very soul,
Kind words are always a click away,
You'll be fine just get through today,
In triumph we count those who matter most,
In victory be the modest host,
Waiting for that incoming call,
Nervous times lingering in the once friendly hall,
Children on their first day of school,
Teach them well behave now don't act the fool,
We all share a common thread,
From a joyous occasion to unwelcome dread,
Whether we bring life in or see it out,
We're not so different, for that there is no doubt.

# Loss & Gain

Ready to speak about your gain,
Comes at a cost of unseen pain,
No one sees the work put in,
Can sit back and quietly grin?

If life is all about winning that toss,
Would you be graceful in defeat and accept your loss,
Is it all down to luck and the roll of the dice?
Gamble it all for a piece of that slice,

Are you richer or poorer by the end of the day?
You never know what might be thrown your way,
Does fortune really favour the bold?
Experience is gained and the truth be told,

Not all wealth is kept in a Bank account,
It's the appreciation of life in its large amount,
Even if you fall at the final fence,
Ultimately you have gained common sense.

# Look Beyond

If you can keep your head,
When all sense has seemingly fled,
When the dogs of judgement bark so loud,
Covered in an angry shroud,
The aim is to drag you down,
To a level of not much renown,
You want to scream and blow a fuse,
Given in to such a ruse,
The Demons of the human spirit,
Taunt and tease to seek false merit,
Then we're left to figure it out,
What the anger was unleashed about,
We all have that fire that wants to erupt,
To silence those who are too abrupt,
We live in an age of violence at the finger tips,
So through our being it firmly rips,
Do we get battle ready and collide head on,
Our faith in decency now truly gone,
For those who seek to wind the wheel
A little of your soul for to steal,
So with the feet planted firmly on the ground,
It is hard to ignore the annoying sound,
The ones who pontificate I'm always right
How do they sleep in the dead of night,
As we wish to slumber with our day done right,
Not a second thought to those who live their life with intended
spite.

# Living Abroad

It comes to stay unannounced,
Feel its grip like a lion has pounced,
What to do or where to go,
When will it end we just don't know,

So now we try to deal with what has occurred,
At the moment it all looks blurred,
Travel away to earn a wage,
In the story of life turn a new page,

Got to go has to be done,
To foreign lands under the hot sun,
Leave behind what was always familiar,
Soon realise you've found something similar,

Takes a while to settle in,
A new lifestyle with a nervous grin,
Think of home when the day's work is done,
You get used to it and have a bit of fun,

Get on the net and put up a post,
Were doing well in a hidden boast,
A life changing event comes your way,
Here for now or here to stay,

If and when you need a break,
Several options you can take,
Can always take the long haul flight,
Be with loved ones by the dawn's early light!

# Is Religion The New Politics?

Be you Pagan, Christian, Gentile or Jew,
Religious beliefs are now under the scope and up for review,
Was it originally intended to put some goodness in the race of
man,
Love one another and do all you can,

Whether you are standing or kneeling at your chosen pew,
Are we born with concept of a blinkered view,
Listen to us and we'll save your soul,
soon caught on to the power of control,

Even though the world is in complete upheaval,
Can religious beliefs be blamed for this evil,
Taking the lives of those who are deemed inferior,
Can they really tell this from a mere exterior,

Downloading footage off the internet,
Evil finds sanctuary where ever it is let,
Our planet is revolving to selfish and immoral greed,
Back in the archive of time was planted this seed,

The media is telling you who to hate,
Then sparks the reason for a heated debate,
The finer things in life are sought after with an insatiable thirst,
When you wake in the morning, what is your priority first,

So in the midst of all this callous behaviour,
Just be a good person for that is the true saviour,
Have respect for the good natured human being,
The gods are watching, the gods are seeing!

# Into The Night

When the night lays down its mortal shroud,
The moon sneaks a peek from under a shining cloud,
It covers the land with a foreboding hush,
Man and beast into the darkness rush,

Not all are content to lay down and sleep,
Into the night into it deep,
The playground for worker and thief,
Dawn sends its awaited relief,

Daytime is a chore and left to the masses,
Night-time is for paly where party goers tip their glasses,
Finding love or just a distraction,
For most the night is a welcome attraction.

# An Impartial View

It's with great unbounding sadness,
That we are plunged into relentless madness,
The sands of time begin to slowly drown,
Any hope of humanity in this never ending slope down,

Divide and conquer is the order of the day,
Careful what you do and watch what you say,
Dedicated to the cause writing the daily page,
It's second nature now, this unbridled rage,

Colour, class, race and creed,
Thrown into the mix, this destructive seed,
If the powers that be are in all their might,
Why are they putting us into a mindless fight,

The human race is almost spent,
The Devil is almost due his rent,
Does a God really exist,
Why allow this lunacy to persist,

Or have we made our bed,
It's welcomed in this demonic dread,
We are quick to blame and point the finger,
We've given evil a home so why wouldn't it linger,

We go around with the best intentions,
The disease is long past any preventions,
We are the puppets on the string,
The foul deeds of others are starting to infect and to sting.

# I'll Just Leave This Here

When the day closes swiftly down,
Have we done enough to escape a frown,
Reflecting on the time that's past,
On time spent a thought is cast,

Have I done enough for tomorrow to find,
Given my all to the daily grind,
My mind is slowly submerged,
Settled nicely or kind of purged,

Didn't read the instructions thought I'd give them a miss,
Carry on in the unrelenting bliss,
Did I do my part in easing mankind along,
Never judge and first do no wrong,

Go through the days like revolving doors,
How many footprints cover these floors,
For I am not alone in this timeless quest,
Asking immortality to be my guest,

So shuffling by on this busy road,
To the endless routine I commend this ode,
What is our greatest fear,
That time would erase what I have done here.

# Against the World

If I roared at the thunder and it answered back,
In making the most noise who would sound the loudest
crack,
If the wind blew a fearsome gale,
Would resistance make me impoverished and pale,
If I put my hand to stop the rain,
Would its downpour only just cause me pain,
If the sun shone bright on its hottest day,
Would I be able to gentle its glow without delay,
If I stood on the ocean's edge,
Try and make myself an unstoppable ledge,
The fearsome power knock me off my feet,
Facing an almost certain defeat,
In this battle with natures onslaught,
A fine lesson would be taught,
Against nature and its force,
It just has to vent and run its course,
If I was faced with a formidable foe,
How to defend and attack, I'd be in the know,
To run and hide or counter and evade,
From villainy sharp as a blade,
We have come to a point in our existence,
To cause each other so much resistance,
Equality on the proclaimers grounds,
Yet in hind sight we know no bounds,
For we are delicate and of fragile means,
Tend to act we are a force of nature so it seems,
The true power of the world is what really is in control,
So, we should play more of a tenants role.

# A Mild Form Of Protest

E choes from our past are shown,
Defiance in its number has grown,
United we will all stand tall,
You won't hit the ground if you fall,

Our forefathers scream for justice from within,
Can't hear us above the deafening din,
To stand up and be counted,
Tension has now being mounted,

Our leaders have failed in their daily chore,
Now we can take no more,
Take to the streets and lets be heard,
Determined no show of force will us be deterred,

United and strong we'll stand together,
For deceit has us at the end of our tether,
Trying to squeeze every last cent that we've got,
Power abused by the entire lot,

Trying to kill our beautiful land,
Paying the piper for every back hand,
North, South, East and west,
In for the long haul, for our nation let's do our best,

No longer the sheep and blindly follow,
The wolves beware the pit of your stomach should feel hollow,
Water is a simple god given right,
Not for crooks to cause an unjust blight!

# Glimpse Of Life

We begin life alone in the womb,
  Then commended for eternity alone in a tomb,
Along way we gather the acquired knowledge,
From playschool till enrolled in college,
Learn to adapt to the social scene,
Get through it intact and immaculately clean,
Make friends and hope their the choices were right,
Sometimes it's tough marred with the odd fight,
Do our best to show good face,
Don't want to be rude or a total disgrace,
Find employment and pay the bills,
When it gets too tough walk softly in between the drills,
Yes there can be cause for aggression,
The mood falls short and into a recession,
The house the car the bank account receipt,
Can't take it with you when life hits delete,
So why are we here and what's it all about,
When in doubt just give it a clout,
Does the daily routine have purpose and reason,
You have to look good it's in this season,
So why is so we live in such fear,
Could it be we'll be forgotten and the world will not have
known we were even here.

# From My View

I was on a hill to experience the view,
The scenery gave me a picturesque clue,
God took his time in creating this place,
Long before the human race,

I walked down the side of the hill,
The birds sang both loud and shrill,
As almost to announce my arrival,
Years of experience has enhanced their survival,

The local wildlife came out to gaze upon my presence,
A sight of almost spectacular pleasance,
I'm only a visitor a passer-by,
From this view so pleasing to the eye.

# Don't Be Hasty...

A lot of unrest it must be said ,
Fingers pointing and furious shaking of the head,
We are not happy at what is going on,
Is the last shred of humanity finally gone,

Copy and paste what we see and feel,
Some how anger has great appeal,
Jump into the fray all guns blazing,
A row over very little is often amazing,

A gap in time, a space to fill,
Get it said, you know the drill,
Jump to a conclusion before knowing the facts,
Patience hung out to dry on the unforgiving racks,

The great retaliation comes quick and fast,
Keyboards clatter with a judgemental blast,
Surely we could have something better to do,
Instead of fuelling this sub-conscious flu,

It's very easy to say what's on your mind,
Sitting as the microchips grind,
Whether it's in an instant or drawn out,
Sometimes the less said is the more sensible route.

# Cryosleep

If tonight i fell asleep,
Fell in and fell very deep,
Woke far from now in a different decade,
What would have this slumber made,
What would greet my eyes at first glance,
in this future circumstance,
Would a shock descend upon my being,
Beholding all that i was seeing,
Would people be less friendly or more inclined,
Has humanity increased or be just declined,
The mode of transport taking to the skies,
Nothing on wheels, now it all flies,
Social media banned or in every aspect more than ever,
Still making a point and look so clever,
Animals reign supreme in their domains,
Extinct maybe like the rains,
Their portraits on screens and walls,
Computer enhanced would be their calls,
Do we know or much long with care,
To speak our minds if we dare,
Days trips to the Moon and Mars,
Museums now displayed with vintage cars,
Will technology be better or worse for our existence,
A form of bone idol lazy resistance,
Who knows or who can tell,
Locked in a trance of this technological spell,
If time travel was all the rage,
Would i be left behind or be wise old sage,
Come back to the night before,
These days that would become folklore,
Would it beggar belief what i have learned,
Or would to remain in the future be forever yearned.

# Social Media

From its creation it's been a blur
Over the years has caused quite a stir,
From trolls, hackers and the haters,
A platform for the great debaters,

From a photo out with some people,
Images of scenery with the highest steeple,
Can't wait to sit and go on line,
A photo of your meal before we dine,

From funny jokes to inspiring quote,
Here's a photo of me in my new coat,
It's all about where you are and what you're at,
In the pub with pint I'm only sat,

Here's a new application,
Casing quite the sensation,
The new wheels I got and it was a steal,
Wow nice motor I bet that was a done deal,

This is my collection took years to hoard,
Look at this Dog on a snowboard,
Can't remember what I did last night,
Did I insult any one or get in a fight,

Some dishes are from sweet to savoury,
Footage of acts of complete and utter bravery,
Two lads punching till one falls down,
Do you comment with angry face or a frown?

Then the row starts over the state we are in,
Times used to be better how long has it been,
Old friends meet after years of not seeing,
I suppose we will always be on social media as the art of
conversation is quickly fleeing.

# So What Now?

The mighty powers go head to head,
While the innocent wind up dead,
Are we about to self-destruct,
Inside this ever changing construct,
Is it about whose dog has the biggest bark,
What deals made with the Devil in the menacing dark,
Keep the human race living in fear,
Seems so when a threat is made so clear,
Are the powers not so super,
Leaving us in a fear induced stupor,
The long since predicted end of days,
Wallowing in a Nuclear haze,
On social media we bicker and troll,
Whose wrong and right, batters the soul,
Chaos has a happy home,
With each angry word, it's allowed to roam,
Long since has it being foretold,
One generation will not grow old,
To see who has the biggest dog in this fight,
Morals and humanity now take flight
Or just the rich and powerful at their daily play,
Keeping us in line and at bay,
It is political and religious views,
Near dying of boredom themselves to amuse,
There is a pattern that has formed throughout the ages,
Our world marred with war, it's in all the the historic pages,
Do they secretly convene to renew their Luciferian vow,
Leaves us to ponder, so what now?

# The Market Place

We strive every morning to make our daily bread,
On those dreaded of days you'd rather stay in bed,
Get up now go punch that clock,
Live life to the fullest every day we rock,

But, a question does come to mind,
When were stressed to the limit of the daily grind,
Is it all worth it and why are we doing this,
Struggling to find mortal bliss,

In this human race do we finish first or last,
Who cares really as long as we have a blast,
Try our best to have a great day,
Whose really in charge who has the last say.

Are we just a commodity with an expiry date,
Get in your life's worth before it's too late,
Are we living within the law,
Seems some are exempt as they live life pure raw,

Where are we shackled on the food chain,
Daily events are now beyond insane,
Do we reside in the fall out zone,
One day the Devil will come to claim his own.

# The Changing Face Of Humanity

If we look at our present times,
Is destiny ringing out the foreboding chimes,
People wired into a technological hub,
Is Narcissism beginning to rub,
Into the minds of every being,
What's now unfolding is beyond believing,
Is the Tsunami of importance about to reign,
Fictional kings and queens in a blurred distain,
A generation spoiled from every wanting notch,
It may well come to an end on their watch,
Shocking behaviour has become the norm,
Pray tell to take shelter in this ever growing storm,
Confused ideals take president over once moral obligations,
Frowned upon now with arrogant complications,
Are we becoming an endangered race,
Confused and baffled by our ever changing social face,
Has simple manners been done away with,
Or deemed too old fashioned from where we sit,
Our existence is no longer sugar coated,
It's now documented the ungrateful never ending and truly
gloated,
It's like a plague spreading like it's the latest trend,
Respect is no longer required, share the message, send,
Lawless, no justice, no peace,
It's growing like a virus and will not cease,
Hell is truly empty or so it would appear,
No horns or hoofs, but all the Devils are most certainly here.

# Think Before You Ink

If life is viewed with the ambiguous gaze,
Casting dispersions in a shrouded haze,
Look from the heart and not from the head,
Make up your own mind and not be easily led,

We all want to live in relative peace,
It comes from within when the inner beast cease,
When our lives are affected,
When a threat is detected,

Jump into an action of complete self-defence,
Look at the bigger picture from that day hence,
The media is full disaster and inhuman crime,
Human nature has processed this since the beginning of time,

Too quick to jump to a ready conclusion,
Sometimes that answer is just disguised confusion,
Get on a social network and have a rant,
It feels like holding tight on a downward slant,

We all have opinions to be freely expressed,
Often it's an observation that probably best,
A comment made in anger can't always be taken back in regret,
Keep a cool head and your heart will be set,

We are all prone to moments of unbridled rage,
Learn from that moment as you turn the next page!

# The Way It Is

We have come to the point in our existence,
Without warning pose as much resistance,
On the defensive night and day,
Repeat that, what did you say,

The saying goes why can't we all just get along,
Do no harm and first do no wrong,
Give your opinion without force or might,
I'm only saying doesn't mean I'm right,

We are all in an insecure location,
We have to be right it's our vocation,
A word a gesture an accidental action,
Cause for uproar an aggressive reaction,

Walking around in self-defence mode,
Watch where you're going obey the code,
We don't rise in the morning hell bent on confrontation,
A good deed a day is cause for elation,

On the road on the street or just sat at the computer,
We are ready to do battle with each and every commuter,
It's got to the point where we want it now,
We have become greedy as a crow behind a plough,

These are the inner workings of the human being,
Now it's everywhere it's getting worse what we're seeing,
I don't think it started out meaning to be anything like this,
It's becoming extinct this mortal bliss,

Once so full of life, flavour and fizz,
It's frightening to say that's reality and the way it is.

# What Matters Most!

It's at certain times you made to reminisce,
Peer into the past with unatoned bliss,
What makes a memory stand out so proud,
What sets it off is deafeningly loud,

A smile, a smell, a chance meeting,
Here in the trophy of mind with the mental greeting,
Some time ago when this took place,
The emotion is written all over your face,

Some struggle to remember the past,
But, the will is set and the dye is cast,
Is it all by choice or some trigger of the mind,
This is the playground of life inside that you find,

Whether it is an event or a simple sound,
The flood gates open at the incoming and out bound,
Are we just passengers or the dedicated participants,
It all comes on all forms regardless of the recipient's,

Some you like to sit alone with them and dream,
They go from the dregs to the absolute cream,
A penny for them we are often tasked,
It's often better to keep them to yourself if you're actually
asked,

Some you hope to forget,
Haunting your memories if they are let,
We often say let's propose a toast,
To the times and joys and to what matters most.

# What Did We Do Before The Internet?

That's a question that's regularly asked,
in anonymity we daily basked,
did you go to the match and what did you think,
went to the pub with the lads to have drink,

It was wondrous word of mouth,
did you meet anyone nice or give an eejit a clout,
a photo was taken to be cherished for all time,
now were flooded daily without reason or rhyme,

We have to know what's happening without delay,
we didn't sit showing off our phones back in the day,
it was a big lump of plastic that sat in the hall,
if you dropped it the ground would be shattered from the force
of the fall,

Now we all sit around in silent retreat,
a room full of people on the edge of their seat,
at the continuous flow of information,
cause for judgement and condemnation,

So, before the art of conversation is completely outdated,
use your mouth to speak before it becomes over rated,
as children we spent years to perfect this art,
now the mouth seems to close when the apps begin to start,

Yes the space age has brought in new ways to better mankind,
it can also leave what we take for granted, too far behind.

# Walking the Road

We all walk a different road,
It's better not to think about your load,
Into the future we must gaze,
Seems to vanish into the distant haze,

Difficult to decide which way to turn,
Your weary feet begin to burn,
The future is never set,
Proceed with caution where to place your life's bet,

Lessons to be learned if you get it right,
The horizon may seem all the more bright,
It's not something you can read from a book,
It's about the journey and the road you took.

# What's On Your Mind?

As we head towards the years end,
Wondering what the new will send,
In reflection of the year that's past,
Those burning bridges not made to last,

What new terror will the world devise,
Send innocent souls to their demise,
It's said great minds think alike,
If you don't think like me, then take a hike,

Too quick to jump to hasty conclusion,
Humanity is suffering from great confusion,
We look to the skies to whatever you name your God,
Does it make any difference when you're interned beneath the
sod,

The years are going so fast,
A good time is not made to last,
Is life really too short,
We answer with a sharp retort,

We celebrate all life's ponderous occasions,
Life and birth and the near death evasions,
So if you have made a milestone this year,
That has set you up from promise to fear,

When you're busy with your chosen graft,
We are odd and often quite daft,
We as beings are capable of great compassion,
Live every day as a daily ration,

We know and have seen great loss,
Would you change it all for a simple coin toss,
So take a moment to contemplate,
The years not over nor is it too late,

Is it all go and too much hassle,
Just be humble not king of the castle,
Now we live at a hectic pace,
But it's not done yet, this human race,

We all have enough to do,
Even if it seems like an endless queue,
Take the time and you will find,
Don't worry too much about what's on your mind!

# This Year's Production: (An Ode)

So the stage was set the lines were learned,
For opening night the cast have yearned,
Waiting patiently backstage,
One last look and turn the page,

Their fearless leader had taught them well,
Remember those lines even if the audience can't tell,
Be on time and ready to go,
Lots to be done before the show,

Will you ever put down that coffee cup
I won't tell you again get to make up,
All fitted for sound and vision,
Deliver those lines with expert precision,

In the darkness of backstage,
Nerves are shredded but it's time to engage
How many are in is asked with anticipation,
Is the main cause for alarm and a little perspiration,

With months of planning that has come to pass,
Now it's time to show some class,
Rehearsals seemed never ending,
Got to get it right the plot needs sending,

For those who worked tirelessly and are not seen on the night,
Are just as dedicated to getting it right,
Even if it's only a two night run,
Put on a performance second to none.

# An Ode To The Martial Artists

We forge our bodies in the fires of our will,
Endless dedication to hone a unique skill,
Relentlessly in our daily quest,
We all want to be the best,

Passed down from the past generation,
not forgetting times of frustration,
Selfless acts of human endeavour,
Outsmart your opponent and always be clever,

One step ahead like a game of chess,
Have respect and accept nothing less,
Whether you punch with a fist or hit with a knee,
Everybody wants to be Bruce Lee,

Doesn't matter who you call master,,
Don't want to be a victim and end up in plaster,
Fight for a prize or just an interest in self-defence,
Protect yourself always makes sense,

Martial arts there are many good instructor there are few,
The ones who see life from a different view,
A sense of wellbeing and self-control,
Dates back to the times when they read from a scroll,

Spirits of warriors that have gone before,
Rekindled in the hearts of the ones who are worthy of folklore,
Whether the art finds the person or the person finds the art,
You'll know it will suit right from the start,
Ego is firmly cast aide, Walk with peace by your side!

# A Bit Political

# Lest We Forget
## 9/11

The day that began like any other,
    Soon the world would stand in a mind numbing shudder,
The face of tyranny came from the sky,
Good souls sent to the sweet bye and bye,

The working day was torn apart,
The question of humanity was about to start,
Lives taken for by an evil torque,
The earth shook all over the state of New York,

The sights that followed were scarcely believable,
Such want and destruction how was it conceivable,
The innocent taken by those who scorn,
Relatives in heads bowed began to mourn,

The devil sits back and admires the view,
Happy and content with evil that men do,
For God created us all to be equal,
If we don't change, the human race may not have a sequel!

# Same Sex Marriage

So we go to the polls today,
Make haste with no delay,
It's being put to a vote,
The right to marry on a high note,

Straight, single, bi or gay,
Time to let the world know what we have to say,
Is it really about an equal right,
About time we shed our own light,

In the country on the last outpost,
That special day do we really need permission to host,
Man or woman does it really matter,
Often it's closed minds make the most clatter,

Today we will all vote yes,
The brides and grooms sent forth to bless,
Take the vow and commit to each other,
Who knows it could be your sister or brother,

Lets get it done and celebrate,
Then with sober heads yesterday's wedding to rate,
We live in age of space exploration,
But ask questions when same sex couples display adoration,

Lets be a shining light across the globe,
Love is love so let's use that common sense between each ear lobe,
So forget for a day about your trouble and strife,
Bring hope to those who yearn for a shared life!

# In The Light Of Recent Events

So the world has now being plunged into crisis,
Fuelled by hate by the evil Isis,
People fleeing in search of a safe haven,
Now the key board warriors have started raving,

It's being evident for thousands of years,
What we see today are confirming the fears,
We have not learned as a human race,
Who we call god and the colour of our face,

If we were all the same the planet would be boring,
Fear and loathing is now soaring,
Has humanity finally become undone,
Are we awaiting the kingdom come,

We constantly judge and go on the defensive,
Our race is failing, it's time to be pensive,
The flood gates have opened is the time almost nigh,
God may no longer sit back and watch his planet die,

It's not about wrong or right,
It's the army of evil who has brought about this fight,
Look into your soul and see what is there,
The truth of conscience may be hard to bear,

Darkness is only the absence of light,
Stand up for the just in this unsightly plight,
Now we all are worried about an impending doom,
Be true in your heart there is still plenty room,

Will blood stain the once green landscape,
Free yourself from these shackles there is an escape,
Evil has ruined this planet for far too long,
This our home too where we truly belong!

# 1916-2016

Today we reflect on those who died,
countless relatives who grieved and cried,
who against the backdrop of Dublin city,
the scenes of war were horrific and gritty,

lives given in a quest to be free,
bodies torn in a merciless melee,
the roar of the canons in the Irish air,
the gruesome sights caused the hardest of hearts to stop and
stare,

skies opened and awaited their arrival,
with the morning dawned a day of survival
didn't matter now who they called god,
the they all went to heaven when the bodies were interned in
the sod,

The fight for freedom and the defence of the crown,
they all laid lifeless in dear old Dublin town.

God bless Ireland and those who fell 100 years ago today.

# For The People Of Gaza!

As bombs rain down on the innocent masses,
Does not distinguish between the social classes,
Humanity has long since failed,
All shred of decency completely impaled,

The evil that men do,
Has happened before and is nothing new,
To let hatred reach such height,
We can only imagine the peoples plight,

Such horrific images on the internet,
A planned attack the time was set,
In our day and age,
Evil has turned over a different page,

Powers that be stand idly by,
How many more children need to die,
You will all know where you were when this took place,
The look of terror on each face,

Man's blind indifference of his fellow man,
We must help and do all can,
A half a world away,
Words have failed, nothing left to say,
Spare a thought if this suffering was mine,
May peace come soon to the nation of Palestine!

# 11th Hour, 11th Day, 11th Month

Silence descended on no man's land,
Cease fire agreed with the pen in hand,
In a railway carriage alone in a clearing,
The signatures from a huddle were peering,
The day before a thunderous roar,
Ripped through the air missiles did soar,
From fixed positions to rain down death,
The war was not over not just yet,
For four long years the battles raged on,
Every resemblance of humanity well and truly gone,
From bullet to boot and bayonet,
A war of attrition in a steadfast net,
Engaging from morning and through every night,
The darkness lit up by the flares light,
To see if the the enemy did advance,
To gain precious yards there may be a chance,
Bombs and barbed wire scorched the earth,
Strangled and choked by the gas insert,
This was the war to put an end to all others,
That wasn't the case when it sent home shell shocked fathers
and brothers,
The ones who start wars never do any of the fighting,
They are good at getting young men's passion igniting
To go off to war and stay where they fall,
Until the battlefield echoes with the last post and call,
Man's blind indifference to his fellow man,
To bring order through chaos is a failed master plan,
Humanity derailed in the disease ridden trenches,
While death takes his seat on the blood soaked benches,

How many wars have happened since it went all quiet on the western front,
War is a merciless pig in which all you can expect is a grunt.

# The Boy On The Beach

The world has now being shocked by this sad scene,
How long has this crisis refused to be seen,
Has the existence of humanity finally failed,
The history of man now derailed,

Setting sail in search of hope,
Freedom being dangled at the end of a rope,
The powers that be can no longer hide,
Truth has being seen and not be denied,

As the race of Adam and eve,
what did we possibly hope to achieve,
A child face down in lonely tide,
Anger and grief we cannot abide,
While greed is allowed to thrive and prosper,
a child does not matter it's not on the roster,
when the great corporations peer into their account,
This child could have being saved for a small amount,

Not how this journey should have ended,
This is never what our creator would have intended,
Spurred on by the evil that men do,
A long line of souls patiently waiting in the celestial queue.

# The Struggle In South Africa

To a great man I would like to pay tribute,
Sent to jail because his views did not suit,
Those in who calmed to be in power,
Wanted to make the black man cower,

27 years in solidarity confinement,
He struggled to keep his spirit in alignment,
Around the world the protests for him to be free,
From a dreary cell, not much could he see,

Made every endeavour not to diminish his soul,
What lay ahead inspired the world as a whole,
The day came when they let him out,
Rejoicing in the streets led people to scream and shout,

All that time they had taken away,
Choose not to be bitter, had a kind word to say,
A country in political upheaval,
Took it on himself to stop the evil,

Held back a violent tide,
Under a system called apartheid,
As the leader of the A.N.C,
He was about to make history,

Elected South Africa's first black president,
To the people became an iconic resident,
Put the past behind and start to forgive,
Black and white together we must live,

In 1995 he answered a new call,
To inspire a team to win a tournament of the oval ball,
We have lived in a time of a great human being,
His likes again we will never be seeing,

You embraced those on the opposing side,
Peace is the path we must all abide,
Rest in peace you amazing man,
You taught us to strive for peace and do all we can!

R.I.P, Nelson Mandela!

# D-Day 1944

The sea beneath their boats churned,
To defeat the enemy they were spurned,
Stomachs sick with fear,
Thoughts of those they held most dear,

Young men in the eve of impending doom,
The defeat of tyranny was about to loom,
Brothers in arms headed for the shore,
The bombardment was a deafening roar,

The ramps went down on the beach,
Past enemy lines they had to reach,
Gun fire rained down on them like hell,
Surviving this day, no one could tell,

Death letter in their pocket,
Cut to shreds by a stray rocket,
All day long men poured on to the battleground,
Alas when it was over, some could not be found,

The world is now what it is to a certain degree,
Thanks to thousands of brave men who gave their lives on
Normandy,
By days end they had broken through,
The immediate horror was an unsightly view,
Humanity was cast aside,
Evil was on the downward slide,

Bad news gone home to each ma,
Ghosts now walk the beach of Omaha,
In the surf each hero lay,
Lest we forget the sacrifice given on D-Day!

# The Constant Battle

As we are all God's creation,
Satan likes to take lives for his recreation,
Doesn't care about colour of skin or origination,
Likes to watch mortals suffer with pure elation,

It matters not what tongue we speak,
The agents of Satan need souls to seek,
A quest that began since the dawn of the human,
Make us fight each other without presuming,

Is it really about colour, race or creed,
It's the root of Evil that enables a callous deed,
So it's made to like the fingers are pointing,
No matter how your faith requires anointing,

Be you Christian, Muslim, Gentile or Jew,
You're a terrorist regardless of your chosen pew,
So, wherever they pick to cause want and destruction,
Another web of deception is under construction.

# My Favourite Game

# Soldier Fields

In a night where expectations were high,
Pride and passion you could not deny,
Was this going to be another defeat of epic proportion,
What was in store, we had no notion,

Went ahead in the early stages,
By the final whistle would rewrite Irish sporting pages,
The Blacks came back to close the gap,
Every ounce of energy it was going to sap,

True grit and determination,
Was going to ignite the whole nation,
As the clock slowly ticked down,
It was going to be an unforgettable night on the town,

For so long we waited for the score to go our way,
History was made on this day,
The Irish rose to their feet all over the world,
As the date with destiny finally unfurled,

For it was only a week before,
We were in mourning, our hearts were sore,
In tribute to their fallen team mate,
They faced the Haka in the figure 8,

The might of New Zealand put us to the test,
In a place called Soldier field we were the best.

# 2015 Rugby World Cup: the world in union!

We enter this life not knowing what fate will decide,
Then your chosen task comes in like the early morning
tide,
Not alone do you answer this call,
If the gods played a game, it would be that of the oval ball,

Find a position and hone your skill,
It's a rush that would make the faintest heart go still,
To be strong and move with amazing grace,
Ball in hand to the line, on is the race,

It's time to focus and do your job,
Get there first, the loose ball to rob,
The hard work is done time to put it to the test,
Giving it your all nothing less than the best,

When we walk on to that hallowed ground,
The surge of adrenaline makes your heart pound,
You know it's about your team mates and the colour on your
back,
Courage and determination no one will lack,

It is only the chosen few who go on to hold the highest
accolade,
A test of endurance to make the all-important grade,
Except the responsibility and all that it bears,
Hold your resolve when others lose theirs,

There can be no denying when you're on this great honourable route,
It's the making or breaking in that moment of truth!

# The Six Nations

So after a long day it's been decided,
The grace of god we have been guided,
Came down to the final game,
Once more claimed six nations fame,

The best tournament on the planet,
The evidence is there as men stepped up as hard as granite,
From each kick and ruck and maul,
Had us on the edge of our seat and entertaining above all,

Dug down deep and found resolve,
Title hopes they had to solve,
It takes men to make a memorable event,
Legends are made when your body is spent,

So now we look to the world cup,
Raise your game were on the up,
Stand up and fight and take on the best,
Ireland are champions take a well-earned rest,

Enough for now another page of Irish sporting history is
recorded,
Take a bow you have been rewarded!

# For What Ails Us

# The Wretched Within

We gaze upon the human condition,
Many a time is cause for rendition,
What bumps around in the corners of the soul,
Are we really in the penthouse or down in the hole,

It's a clash of consciousness, that keeps us reeling,
We are perfect or that is the feeling,
The voices that drone on under ceaseless attack,
Are they our mentor or just a quick route to the sack,

We get to a point when we know it all,
Do we really it's better than an embarrassing fall,
Has it been proven it's all in your head,
The Demons are relentless as they gather at the foot of the
bed,

Are we just making do in a life relived,
A chance to go back for all the negativity to be sieved,
So, are we in heaven or are we in hell,
Sometimes it's so blurred it's hard to tell,

The beast is not quiet and won't be restrained,
Take a break my foe I am deeply pained,
The struggle continues on a daily routine,
Thoughts are worth gold or so it would seem,

Was Dante really about comedy but far from divine,
Is this our lot be every moment thine.

# For World Mental Health Day

Now we have a day to mental health dedication,
doing our bit full of elation,
When the clock hits midnight it starts all over again,
All day the negativity does reign,

It doesn't take a day off or punch a card,
Feels like your brain is cut to bits by an invisible shard,
The Demons are relentless and do not want your emancipation,
There was a time when the disease of the mind was taboo,
Depression was a word every day would rue,

You can't shut the voices up or turn off the on switch,
It's a constant battle torn down by every mental stitch,
Ah pull yourself together stop looking for attention,
Your emotions reeling from this mental detention,

From the deepest dungeon of your darkest despair,
Alone in the night no refuge to be found there,
People caught up in the daily struggle,
On to your face a smile to smuggle,

But, times have changed we've come a long way,
Now it takes up a whole day,
No more in miscommunication,
Now that's worth celebrating and cause for oration,

So if you still think mental illness is hard to define,
You wouldn't last a day in this world of mine,
Never think you're vindicated or exempt,
It can hit anyone at any time and with utter contempt.

# Cancer

It's the news we all dread to hear,
Especially when it's someone dear,
Do all you can and always be there,
Head in hands, this just isn't fair,

Just sit and listen to how they feel,
Inside you start to reel,
Down inside their very being,
Muster the courage, it's always worth seeing,

When you fall apart at the impending doom,
The sufferer is usually the strongest person in the room,
Lets stand together and put up a good fight,
For those who are ill, be a shining light,

Bravery is a sight to behold,
Even though it would leave you cold,
Feeling we can't find something to do,
Days like this cancer will rue,

For those who are still fighting hard,
We'll all be as one deadly shard,
Those who now rest in the other place,
When we think of courage we'll see their face.

# Cancer Awareness

It is the scourge of our humanity,
A disease that is utter insanity,
Held in the devils grip of fear,
From his lair with an evil leer,

We rally together and do our best,
Raise cash for each and every test,
For a cure we must find,
A noose for cancer lets tightly bind,

We support those who have this dreaded curse,
Open your hearts along with your purse,
United we will all stand strong,
The fight will be hard and long,

For everyone life is a roll of the dice,
Every charity event and that bucket of ice,
We show we care and no one is alone,
Cancer is cruel and as cold as stone,

Do your bit and show some love,
The odd few words to the man above,
Lets sharpen our swords and prepare for battle,
Lets kick cancers arse and give it a good rattle,

To all friends near and far and beyond,
Through acts of kindness we all form an unbreakable bond!

# Remember Way Back Then

# The School Bus

Standing by the roadside on that winters morn,
Looking down and feeling forlorn,
Thinking about the dreaded day ahead,
Why couldn't I just stay in bed,

So the bus rattles round the bend,
Have no pencil, might get someone to lend,
As that wagon grounds to a halt,
The teachers are waiting to ate you without salt,

Stand in the corner if you got it wrong, not much to say,
Just want to see the end of the day,
In doorways and shops we all meet up,
The flask is broken and missing the cup,

Get through the day as best we can,
To bus that evening, we always ran,
The moods all changed as the schools are out,
Pulling and dragging school bags thrown about,

The uniform is a shadow of its morning self,
Launched with delight to the top shelf,
Whose playing tonight and will ya score,
I'm not togging out my knees too sore,

The noise is a deafening roar,
On The bus home hear the decibels soar,
Like a wild herd of buffalo sweeping across the plain,
A pea shooter puts your eye in pain,

The excitement is electric the bus driver is mad,
The best days of our lives we ever had,
For all you parents sending your children off to school,
Don't misbehave or act the fool,

We know how it feels because we were there,
These are the memories that are all too rare.

# Those Lazy Days

The sun shines down to good effect,
Time to get the bbq out the cook to elect,
In the company of good friends,
A meeting feel good messages it sends,

Look to the sky with an approving gaze,
As the warmth sets up a hypnotic haze,
Talk about summers gone by,
A pause for silence with a reminiscent sigh,

Cherish this time filled with bright sunshine,
The living is easy, there's no denying,
Take time out and take stock,
Absorb the moment in your memory lock,

No more teachers, no more books,
Maybe the odd bosses dirty looks,
For it is time to let the good times roll,
The food of life is in your bowl,

Forget about the dreaded recession,
Give friends a call, let's start the session,
The sights and sounds fill up your senses,
Paint the house or repair the fences,

Sit back and leave work for another day,
A little bit longer let's keep reality at bay,
It's a time of year that is sublime,
I wish you all the happiness of the summertime!

# A Little Bit Of  Home

# The Golden Fleadh

As the days brighten up and send more light,
The parish on the suir is a pleasant sight,
With any event that fills the night air with sound,
Take your time and stroll around,

You can always walk at your own pace,
A ready 'how's the going' from any familiar face,
Even though hard times has decreased us in size,
We all know where our heart truly lies,

Whether it's home for the weekend or a longer break,
It's not always about time or how long you have to take,
Just to be there and soak it all up,
Treasure each moment and sip every sup,

Now if you live far away over the churning foam,
It may not be easy to read this poem,
All you need to do is close your eyes and bow your head,
You'll be there in an instant and that's enough said!

# The Athassel Abbey

It sits on the banks of the Suir river,
In times gone by the winter wind caused quite a shiver,
Its ruins stretching across the sands of time,
Surrounded by the landscape of a rich deep lime,

As children we played till it got dark,
when it comes into view it ignites a spark,
Many a summers day we whiled away the hours,
Ran for cover from thunder showers,

If you shared an experience in this timeless place,
From the heart puts a smile on your face,
It was home to dwellers long ago,
Had a simple life rich soil for crops to grow,

It's as symbolic as our little village,
Monks tended the land and prepared the tillage,
Made a life that was far removed from the comforts we have
today,
Stand on the road and history is all around you in a fine array!

# The Castle On The Bridge

It stands alone from times gone by,
like a sun dial stretching to the sky,
to see it in the morning haze,
the sunshine in its panoramic blaze,

people pass it regularly day to day,
some stop and spend a while to stay,
where men kept watch with daily chore,
the green landscape to the fore,

On the island was it chosen ground,
built it beside the Suir waters sound,
it may not be a wonder of this earth,
but, it's a landmark of noble birth!

# The River

Meandering in its graceful motion,
On its way to the vast ocean,
Passing through cities, towns and the odd village,

For some it is a way of life,
Living on the river has its trouble and strife,
A weekend getaway to relax the mind,
Sit, watch and listen, an ideal way to unwind,

Sometimes it unleashes its wrath,
Bursting its banks and adding a destructive path,
Meaning harm is not its intention,
We get in the way and it feels like extinction,

For millions of years since it first had its birth,
Its contents cover nearly half of the earth,
Holding all life in its graceful grip,
When thirsty it provides a nourishing sip.

# Seasons

# Springtime

When the winter shrugs off its chilling shroud,
   The days start to stretch and roll back each cloud,
The birds cheer in the change with a joyful song,
To ease the days gently along,

The artic rain continues to fall,
Till soon enough snow graces each and every wall,
The hills have a matching blanket of white,
Now it's passing since it was all a night,

The frost clings on to where it previously rested,
Ice is breaking the resistance has been tested,
A brisk breeze laps across your face,
Caught in the last of winters embrace,

A fog of breath is visible in the morning air,
The rising sun with its blinding glare,
Peers in the window of once a dark dawn,
Emerging from the seasons yawn.

# The Siberian And Emma

They met in the stratosphere,
Two weather fronts that was quite severe,
Came rolling in with storm force power,
The ice man Comet to chill each and every hour,

Backed up by his one night stand,
Not for 30 years have we seen its brand,
Haven't seen the Galtee's for days,
Completely lost in this Artic haze,

From panic buying going out of our head,
It was almost chaotic the shortage of bread,
Get the fire on and don't let it go out,
If you do you'll get a clout,

Stay indoors and don't put yourself at risk,
Who'd want to go out, it was quite brisk,
We weathered the worst of the cold blast,
The Siberian and Emma are now the past,

So, then it was out to enjoy what was presented,
In many ways it was resented,
With delays and hold ups to cancellations,
Brought joy to every child's expectations,

The sight though was something to behold,
In the calm what we did unfold,
Delves down deep into the imagination,
Even gives good cause for a little oration.

# St. Paddies Day

It's time again to paint the town,
Put on a big silly hat and act the clown,
Even though we're in recession,
It still won't stop the mighty session,

If you come from the land of green,
Get on the streets it's time to be seen,
Fill your glass and raise a toast,
To country we love the most,

So if you're far from the emerald isle,
Think of home and give a smile,
Make too much noise and get abuse,
Politely say,
*I'M IRISH, WHAT'S YOUR FECKING EXCUSE?!*

# Those School Days

It now all seems like a haze,
thinking back to those school days,
No I phones or internet,
The art of conversation was a safe bet,

Our whole lives lay ahead of us,
Stood around talking waiting for the bus,
Although it seemed that time did drag,
Out to the bike shed for a quick fag,

Passing notes of correspondence,
Get caught and you had to write a repeated sentence,
End of term you sit and quietly beg,
Watch out for that shower of egg,

Get there on time with homework done,
The excuses were second to none,
Weather it was the Convent, Tech or the brothers,
If you went to one you didn't forget the others,

We got schooled in a different time,
It was never about the social ladder climb,
We would all meet at lunchtime for the craic,
No matter your uniform we watched each other's back,

The teachers ruled and be in no doubt,
Many a cauliflower ear from many a clout,
These days did eventually had to end,
On the path of life our own message to send,

The old made way for the new,
We still remember our teenage view,
We have all moved on,
In our hearts those days are never gone,

Looking back now all grown up,
We took a cherished sip of that great cup,
Some grew up to be a parent,
Pay tax and make sure you had the rent,

Weather residing settled down at home,
Long distance across the great sea foam,
Busy now with the daily grind,
to reminisce always time to find,

Brought together to share common bond,
when we were young and what made us respond,
Our hearts begin to soar,
Spare a thought for our dear friends who sadly are not with us
anymore!

# In The Summer Days Gone By

The summer time casts back my mind,
To great days where memories bind,
The days never seemed to end,
Fishing in the river, rod starting to bend,

Sunshine brought eternal bliss,
Those treasured days we now reminisce,
Farmers meeting after 11o'clock mass,
'Give us a hand to knock some grass'

Looking at the sky with disdain,
For god sake, no sign of feckin rain,
We all meet up, the usual gang,
On the way to the river, sometimes we sang,

The care free days of the young,
Songs of old, were usually sung,
Tonight is the first round of the cup,
We'll have to see who'll turn up,

We never knew what was in store,
Talk about the future, don't make me snore,
Jump into the water, the cold would hit,
It'll be grand, once you get used to it,

Scream and shout, a fight might break out,
Nothing serious, it's what it's all about,
Playing cork on Sunday, do you think we'll win?
To say no would be a sin,

Those days we look back with a reflective tear,
Got to be the best time of the year!

# A Change Of Season

The evenings have begun to draw in,
Winter is Autumn's next of kin,
The darkness subsides to reveal a short daylight,
Feeling the north wind's bite,

The winter woolies are down from the attic,
The harsh breeze causes a motion of static,
Head down get where you're going,
Would have stayed at home if I was in the knowing,

Leaves scatter all around the ground,
The natural litter is everywhere to be found,
The landscape covered in a glistening white,
Left behind by the dead of night,

The summer is now a memory with its cool shade,
There is an unmistakable tint of jade,
Dark clouds gather to deliver its contents,
The mountains take shape like snow covered tents,

It is not all dark and foreboding,
The joy of nature is there for decoding,
The fireside is a welcome haven,
Feel the dusk as dark as a raven!

# All Ireland Day

First Sunday in September,
   A day to forget or one to remember,
On the hallowed ground hope fortune will favour the bold,
Let the victors be wearing the blue and gold,

Paid the money and well worth the cash,
To witness the heart pounding clash of the ash,
Not paid at all ,but,
for honour and glory,
In years to come tell the kids this story,

We'll all hoist the colours and hoist them high,
A 100% we'll hear the battle cry,
Hurl into them and don't stand back,
On this day courage will not be slack,

So come the premier and show some flair,
By milking time we'll have some shiny silverware!

# Winter's Chill

With the trace of autumn truly gone,
Hungry birds ring out their song,
Winter woollies have being dug out,
Minus degrees gives your ears a clout,

See your breath on the icy air,
The dark evenings are cause for despair,
Chain saws echo in the distance,
Christmas is ushered in with little resistance,

Rushing around to get things done,
Get the deep freeze stocked second to none,
It's time for the bargains and get the best deal,
Go on line pay the deposit for it's a steal,

We forget what matters most,
Having family round and being the perfect host,
The coming together and squash them all in,
Just one more mince pie wouldn't want them to end up them in
the bin.

# Wintertime

Good to feel the winter breeze,
In days gone by skating on ponds that did freeze,
The ice flickered in the noon day sun,
The sound of the river flowing by,
Branches on the bottom gently lie,

The fog from a chilled breath,
Keep the hands in the pockets, out the cold will not let,
The swallows have long since gone to foreign climes,
The crows now the only natural chimes,
The castle cast a lazy shadow down,

Clouds gather over to cast a frown,
Light the fire and stay inside,
A good stack of blocks by the fireside,
The days will soon brighten up,
For now keep the kettle boiled for the hot sup!

# Christmas Day

Peace on earth and good will,
Hope your hearts get their fill,
Joy to the world on this day,
It's easy to have a good word to say,

May god shine down on hopes new,
See the world from a different view,
Christ was born in Bethlehem,
To spread some good and stop the mayhem,

Lets all go forward with this in mind,
A better world we will find!
It only comes round once a year,
Time to have loved ones near,

To laugh and sing and be merry,
Whether you came by bus, plane or the ferry,
Block out the cares for a little while,
Be in the company that will make you smile,

Be grateful for the time that has being,
What you have done and what you have seen,
To breathe a deserved sight of relief,
It's being a tough year that beggars belief,

To all friends and family, I wish you well,
Think of you all at the ringing of the bell,
Can't help but to reminisce,
The wonder of such yuletide bliss!

Lightning Source UK Ltd.
Milton Keynes UK
UKHW020620280719

346871UK00008B/303/P